Dealing [illegible] Your Dismissal in a week

ADRIAN BERRY

Hodder & Stoughton

A MEMBER OF THE HODDER HEADLINE GROUP

The Institute of Management (IM) is the leading organisation for professional management. Its purpose is to promote the art and science of management in every sector and at every level, through research, education, training and development, and representation of members' views on management issues.

This series is commissioned by IM Enterprises Limited, a subsidiary of the Institute of Management, providing commercial services.

Management House,
Cottingham Road,
Corby,
Northants NN17 1TT
Tel: 01536 204222;
Fax: 01536 201651
Website: http://www.inst-mgt.org.uk

Registered in England no 3834492
Registered office: 2 Savoy Court, Strand,
London WC2R 0EZ

Orders: please contact Bookpoint Ltd, 39 Milton Park, Abingdon, Oxon OX14 4TD. Telephone: (44) 01235 400414, Fax: (44) 01235 400454. Lines are open from 9.00–6.00, Monday to Saturday, with a 24 hour message answering service.
Email address: orders@bookpoint.co.uk

British Library Cataloguing in Publication Data
A catalogue record for this title is available from The British Library

ISBN 0 340 780924

First published 2000
Impression number 10 9 8 7 6 5 4 3 2 1
Year 2004 2003 2002 2001 2000

Cover photograph from Telegraph Colour Library.

Typeset by SX Composing DTP, Rayleigh, Essex.
Printed in Great Britain for Hodder & Stoughton Educational, a division of Hodder Headline Plc, 338 Euston Road, London NW1 3BH by Cox & Wyman Ltd, Reading, Berkshire.

CONTENTS

INTRODUCTION

This book is intended to help you see what can be done if you are dismissed or made redundant. It is meant to give you a basic outline of what you need to know and what you must do to uphold your rights. It is not meant to be relied upon as legally authoritative. Considerations of space do not permit full treatment of the legal issues. It should serve as a guide so that you may assess your position and see what you need to do to bring a claim. If you are to represent yourself at a Tribunal hearing this book provides you with information on how to obtain legal information and advice and examples of the sorts of questions you should be asking an advisor beforehand.

Throughout the book the Employment Tribunal is known simply as the Tribunal. Further, the book is addressed to 'you' as the 'employee' although there may be situations, as explained, where you are not an employee in law. There are also occasional case citations for the Industrial Cases Reports (ICR) and the Industrial Relations Law Reports (IRLR). In general, legal citation of cases and statutes has been avoided, however cases may well be referred to in a hearing and you should be familiar with the systems used. Throughout the book masculine pronouns have been used to refer to people. No gender specific meaning is intended.

This week we will cover:

Sunday	The Employment Tribunal
Monday	Your employment contract
Tuesday	Wrongful dismissal
Wednesday	Unfair dismissal
Thursday	The remedies for unfair dismissal
Friday	Redundancy
Saturday	Next steps

The Employment Tribunal

If you are not represented by a lawyer or an advisor at a hearing it can be daunting to face your employer who may have employed a solicitor or even a barrister to represent him. Don't feel that you can't meet their standards of preparation. Firstly, not all lawyers prepare cases to exacting standards. Check what they have done against what they ought to have done. Secondly, if you take care you too can bring your case in a thorough and professional manner. The Tribunal hearing your case will understand that you are representing yourself.

This section has been divided into stages:

1. The venue: where to bring a claim
2. How to start a claim
3. Making a settlement with your employer and avoiding a hearing
4. Preparation for the main hearing: what needs to be done
5. What happens at hearings before the main hearing?
6. The ways in which a case may be shortened or determined before a full hearing of the claim
7. The full hearing, introducing evidence and the result
8. What happens afterwards?
9. Next steps

The venue: where to bring a claim

All the types of claim considered here may be brought in an Employment Tribunal. Breach of contract claims, including wrongful dismissal, can also be made in a County Court.

A full Tribunal consists of a chairman (a qualified lawyer) and two non-lawyers who are drawn from a panel representing employers' interests and from a panel representing employees' interests. If a Tribunal is to sit with only a chairman and one non-lawyer, or only a chairman, and you want a full Tribunal because there is a dispute about the facts, ask for one.

How to start a claim

You should send your claim to the nearest appropriate Employment Tribunals Office. There is a list of them in the 'Saturday' section. A claim can be made in any form but it is a good idea to use the standard form called an IT1. Using this form will help you to see what information is required.

You are the Applicant in the case. Your employer is the Respondent. He will receive a copy of your IT1 from the Tribunal. When he receives the IT1 your employer has 21 days to respond by sending an IT3 notice to the Tribunal. Your employer may send an IT3 late and ask for an extension of time. If this is not granted he will not have a defence to the action. For an extension he needs to satisfy the Tribunal that there were reasons for the delay. The Tribunal then considers the relative prejudice you may suffer if the extension of time is allowed against the prejudice your employer will suffer if it is refused.

To amend your IT1 you must apply to the Tribunal. If you want to add another type of action, see whether the time limit for this has expired. If so, make an application for an extension of time. A Tribunal will decide whether to agree to your amendment by considering how major or minor the amendment is, the prejudice that may be suffered in granting or refusing the application, and what reasons there are for the delay and for putting the case in this new way.

Once the Tribunal has received the IT3 it contacts you with the date of the main hearing. Before this date there will often be occasions when you will need to make pre-hearing applications. These are discussed below.

How long do I have in which to bring a claim?

Wrongful dismissal Three months from your effective date of termination ('EDT'). If the EDT cannot be identified, this period runs from your last day of work. A claim for wrongful dismissal may also be brought in the County Court where the time limit is six years.

Unpaid wages Make a claim to the Tribunal within three months of the last occasion on which wages were deducted. The Tribunal may extend this time upon application.

Unfair dismissal Three months from the EDT to make a claim to the Tribunal. For an application after three months you must show that it was not reasonably practical for you to make a claim within three months and that the extra time is reasonable.

Redundancy Six months from the 'relevant date' (the same as the EDT) to make a claim to the Tribunal. If you are late making a claim but are within the next six months, a Tribunal may, on hearing the reasons for the delay and the other relevant circumstances, make an award if it is 'just and equitable' to do so.

The effective date of termination ('EDT') If your job is terminated without notice and notice was not required, then the EDT is the day on which termination occurs. On the other hand, if you are given notice, or you should have been given notice, then the EDT is the day when the period of time specified by, or required as, notice expires.

Making a settlement with your employer and avoiding a hearing

Sometimes it is better to make a settlement. You can ask for things that a Tribunal cannot order such as an agreed reference. If you think you have a weak case it may be better to make a deal with your employer who may be keen to avoid the cost of litigation. In reaching an agreement you eliminate the risk of losing your case and receiving nothing. Any settlement you reach will not result in the Department of Social Security recouping benefits paid to you before the hearing. However if you have been badly treated or humiliated it may be important to try and get a Tribunal verdict declaring that you have been unfairly dismissed, despite the risks.

The time for presenting your claim runs from the date of your dismissal. A crafty employer will spin out negotiations to avoid a claim. Work out the day on which you were dismissed (EDT). Keep a close eye on this date. To protect yourself in case negotiations fail you could start a claim by sending off an IT1 within the time limit. If you are pursuing an internal appeal against dismissal, remember that it is not the date of your internal appeal hearing that counts but rather the date on which you were dismissed. To protect your rights you could issue a claim.

ACAS

When a case comes before a Tribunal it is also referred to the Advisory, Conciliation, and Arbitration Service ('ACAS'). They have a duty to try and reach a settlement. Your ACAS officer can put the terms of any prospective agreement to your employer. If you make an agreement through ACAS you will not be able to bring a further claim on this matter. Where relations between you and your employer are hostile, using ACAS makes it easier to deal with the situation.

An agreement with your employer through ACAS will be set out in a form called a 'COT3'. An employer will often try to have the agreement worded so as to prevent all further claims arising from these facts. If you think that you may have a further claim, such as one for personal injury, make

sure that any agreement you sign allows you to pursue this claim later.

Compromise agreements

You can make an agreement without ACAS. This agreement is known as a compromise agreement. By law it must meet the following conditions:

1. it must be in writing
2. it must relate to the particular complaint
3. the employee must have received advice from a 'relevant independent adviser' as to the terms and effect of the proposed agreement and in particular its effect on his ability to pursue his rights before a Tribunal
4. when the advice is given the advisor must have an insurance policy or an indemnity in force, provided for members of a profession or professional body, in respect of their advice
5. the agreement must identify the advisor
6. it must state that the conditions regulating compromise agreements under the relevant Statute are satisfied.

A 'relevant independent advisor' may be a qualified lawyer, a certified trade union official, or a certified advice centre worker.

Using a relevant independent advisor in order to make a compromise agreement need not be a great expense. Go to an advice centre or a law centre. They may be able to help you. If you are a member of a trade union ask them.

It is also possible for the Tribunal to make an order that approves the terms of the settlement on the day of the hearing.

Preparation for the main hearing: what needs to be done

We will look at:

- Witnesses
- Disclosure of documents
- Further particulars
- Written questions and answers
- Preparing bundles of documents for the hearing
- Witness statements
- What to do if you need more time.

Witnesses

Ask the people you want to give evidence to attend. Consider first whether their evidence is helpful or harmful. Someone may be unwilling to attend because he still works for your employer. The Tribunal can order a witness to attend. An application to the Tribunal for an order to require attendance may be made by letter. The Tribunal will need to know the name and address of the witness. It will consider the relevance of the witness's evidence. The witnesses' expenses in travelling to the hearing and some compensation for loss of earnings are reimbursed from public funds.

Disclosure of documents

If you require documents from your employer to prove your case, write a letter to them and ask for them. If he chooses not to supply them to you, make an application to the Tribunal. You should state in your letter why you think the documents are relevant to the proceedings and necessary to ensure fairness.

Further particulars
If the IT1 form (your form) or the IT3 form (your employer's form) is considered to be insufficient by the other party, a request for further particulars can be made. This occurs when the particular information that identifies the claim being made, or the ground relied upon for making it, requires further development so that the other party to the action can know what the opposing argument will be at the hearing. In an unfair dismissal claim your employer may say that you were dismissed but that you were dismissed for a fair reason. If this is his case, he should state what the reason is and what facts he relies upon in this regard.

Written questions and answers
These are not restricted to developing the matters contained in the IT1 or the IT3. If there is some fact that would help to clarify matters make a request to your employer by letter. If you have not received an adequate answer from him, ask the Tribunal for an order for a written answer. The aim here is to obtain facts to be relied upon, not evidence in support of these facts. Keep a copy of any informal requests you make to your employer and send a copy to the Tribunal if applying for an order.

Preparing bundles of documents for the hearing
Tribunals are frequently confronted with a mass of documents at hearings. The side that presents its case well will have a better chance of impressing the Tribunal with the merits of its case. Put all the documents and correspondence together in chronological order. Give this bundle page numbers and prepare an index showing at which page the documents begin in the bundle. Do not put letters in that are 'Without Prejudice' letters; such as letters between you and your employer where

you are attempting to reach a settlement. Make enough copies of the bundle so there are copies for each member of the Tribunal, an extra for the person giving evidence and a copy each for you and your employer. It may be possible to agree a joint bundle of documents with your employer. If so, make sure you put all the documents in this bundle that you want to rely on. Your employer may well make the copies of this bundle necessary for the hearing and this could save you considerable expense in photocopy charges.

Witness statements

It will help a great deal if you can prepare these. Each witness should draw up his own statement. The statement should deal with all the matters of which the witness has knowledge. A Tribunal can order the exchange of witness statements but this will often be done informally before the hearing.

What to do if you need more time

The Tribunal should give you at least 14 days notice of the date of the main hearing. Usually there is a substantially longer period. If you need more time, ask for it stating the reason why. The Tribunal has the power to adjourn and postpone the hearing. If you ask for more time on grounds of ill-health, either yours or that of an important witness, supply a doctor's note.

You can also ask for a longer hearing. Remember you will be questioning all the witnesses and making speeches. Work out how much time you think you and your opponent will need and ask for more time if necessary.

What happens at hearings before the main hearing?

There are two types of hearing before the main hearing:

- preliminary hearings
- pre-hearing reviews.

Preliminary hearings
This is an opportunity to deal with a discrete issue such as whether the time limits for bringing a case have been observed. Either party may apply for one or the Tribunal may decide that one is necessary. You should ask to have a full tribunal of three people if the case has complicated facts. Be prepared to call evidence as required as if it were the full hearing.

Pre-hearing reviews
You can make an application for a pre-hearing review or a Tribunal may simply decide that one is necessary. Reviews are applied for when one party thinks the other party's case lacks the basis for success and has no reasonable prospects of success at a full hearing. At the review, the way the case is set out is considered rather than actual evidence.

If the Tribunal decides that one party has no reasonable prospects of success it will order that party to pay a deposit of up to £150 in order to continue, after having made enquiries as to the ability of that party to pay. There will be 21 days to pay, which may be extended. The deposit will only be forfeited if you lose and are ordered to pay costs.

The ways in which a case may be shortened or determined before a full hearing of the claim

There are two principle ways in which a case may be shortened or determined prior to a full hearing:

- striking out vexatious pleadings
- striking out pleadings for failing to comply with an order.

Striking out vexatious pleadings
The Tribunal retains a power to determine the case without hearing the parties if the legal issue has been decided in a previous case, or without hearing the respondent if the IT1 does not ask for an appropriate remedy. An IT1 or an IT3 may also be struck out if it is scandalous, frivolous, or vexatious or if the party relying on it is behaving in such a manner. Use these provisions to your advantage against your employer if he is pursuing the case in a frivolous manner either by his conduct or in the IT3.

Striking out pleadings for failing to comply with an order
If either you or your employer fails to comply with an order made in respect of the pre-trial matters, you run the risk of having your IT1 (or, in the case of your employer, the IT3) struck out in part (where the order related to a specific part of your claim) or in full. This means that you will have no case in relation to the parts that have been struck out. If your employer asks for a fine to be imposed on you for failure to comply with an order, make submissions to the Tribunal that this is an extremely oppressive way for them to conduct the case and that a fine is unfair given your resources.

The full hearing, introducing evidence and the result

The hearing

On the day of the hearing arrive at least an hour before you are due to start. Go to the main desk in the reception area and let them know you have arrived. Make sure you know which room you are in by checking the list. In the Tribunal building where your case will take place there are two waiting rooms: one for Applicants and one for Respondents. Give the bundles you have prepared for others and the names of your witnesses to the usher for your case.

At the hearing you will sit at the front on the right hand side as you face the Tribunal. Although in practice few members of the public are likely to attend, they may do so. In Employment Tribunals you stay seated when you are presenting your case. In practice this allows you to find papers quickly and feel less exposed. Witnesses swear an oath or make an affirmation before giving evidence.

The order the hearing takes will depends on what is being disputed. In unfair dismissal cases where the employer admits there was a dismissal, it is the employer who starts first. If the dismissal is disputed then it will fall to you as the employee to prove the fact of the dismissal and thus to begin proceedings. After submissions on dismissal the fairness of the decision will fall to be considered.

In an unfair dismissal case where the dismissal is admitted your employer goes first making an opening speech on the reason for dismissal and the fairness of the dismissal. You then have an opportunity to make an opening speech (opening speeches are often abbreviated or skipped over).

After this the witnesses give evidence. If your employer started the case then his witnesses are called first. Each is questioned by him and then you in turn. Once the Tribunal has heard from all the employer's witnesses it will be the turn of your witnesses. This time you will question them first and then it will be your employer's chance. You will also be giving evidence. When you are giving evidence you will be cross-examined by your employer or his representative. After this you will make the first closing speech and your employer, who made the first opening speech, will make the last closing speech. (Whoever makes the first opening speech makes the last closing speech.)

An opening speech should outline what issues are in dispute, what your version of events is, and the key points that support your case. Illustrate your case by showing the Tribunal which documents you are relying on. In your closing speech you should be aiming to show how the evidence you rely on backs up your points. Do not repeat the evidence. Use it selectively so as to leave the Tribunal with the memory that there is evidence to back up your strongest submissions. Explain to them that your evidence should be preferred. Make your submissions clear and well-defined. Finally, if there is a dispute on the law between you and your employer, this is the moment for you to make your legal submissions. See an advisor if you are thinking of doing this yourself. If you are going to use a law report of a specific case make photocopies of it for the Tribunal.

Introducing evidence

There are principles about the way in which questions are put to witnesses. Be aware of the difference between open questions, such as When . . . ? Why . . . ? How . . . ?

Where . . . ? What happened . . . ? which you ask when questioning your own witness, and leading questions of the type 'You didn't try to find him another job, did you?' which you should ask when cross-examining the employer's witnesses.

Examining your own witnesses is known as examination-in-chief. When you are asking them questions, you should be trying to get them to give their account of what happened and how you were treated. Ask them open questions so that they describe the story in their own words. Do not worry about always asking open, non-leading questions instead of leading questions when you are examining your own witnesses. The Tribunal will know that you are not legally trained.

When you are cross-examining your employer's witnesses you should ask leading questions. Cross-examination of a witness comes after the Tribunal has heard the witnesses story as examination-in-chief. You will not need to go through the same things they have already said again. Instead try and qualify what they have said. If you think about it, they have given evidence for your employer which is hostile to your case. In cross-examining them you should ask questions that add information to the evidence that they have given in ways which help your case. Look to see what they have missed out or have passed over in haste.

Furthermore, ask some questions that undermine the credibility of the evidence being given by the other side so that the Tribunal are more likely to prefer your evidence. Ask questions that show that the witness has made inconsistent statements. Make sure you ask them what actions they took in the light of the things they say they knew. It is very often the case that witnesses will make statements that support their case but that their actions or past behaviour suggests that they are not being truthful.

The result

The decision can be unanimous or by majority. You will be given short or summary reasons. Ask for full reasons if you lose and are intending to appeal. The Tribunal, having decided the issues in the case, will then go on to consider compensation if you are successful. This may be postponed until another day.

What happens afterwards?

The Tribunal will have to decide the matter of costs. A costs order will only be made against the losing party where that party has acted in a vexatious or frivolous manner. A costs order made in such a situation is unlikely to exceed £500. If you lose your case, costs are in issue and you have modest means, you should remind the Tribunal that they must take your ability to pay into account. If you win and are awarded compensation, your employer should pay the sum promptly. If they do not pay, you will be able to enforce the award through the County Court.

Next steps

If you lose your case, there are two ways of continuing the action:

- a review
- an appeal.

Review
If you think there is an error in procedure or there was an omission of evidence and that this has affected the decision, consider a review before the Tribunal. An application must be made within 14 days of the hearing or at the hearing itself.

Appeal
If you think a Statute has been wrongly understood or the decision in favour of your employer is perverse on the evidence available, consider an appeal to the Employment Appeal Tribunal ('EAT'). You have 42 days from when you receive your full reasons from the Tribunal to appeal. Legal Aid is available in some circumstances for representation.

Your employment contract

An employment contract is more than a written statement contained in a single document. It has many sources. In this section we will be looking at:

1. The definition of a contract for employment
2. Terms which are implied into a contract
3. Terms which are expressly stated
4. The role of collective agreements
5. Terms incorporated by Parliament
6. Renegotiating the terms of an employment contract

The definition of a contract for employment

A contract of employment is a special type of contract. It is a contract of 'service' rather than for 'services'. There is a relationship between the employer and the employee beyond that present in a traditional commercial contractual situation. An employer may assert that your contract is not an 'employment contract'. This is because employees have rights that those who merely provide services do not, such as the ability to bring claims for redundancy and unfair dismissal.

The difference between an employment contract and a contract for services is that under the former the employee will serve his employer whereas in a contract for services there is a more limited agreement to provide specified services. In an employment contract, there must also be what is known as mutuality of obligation between the employee and the employer. This means that there are legal obligations that each owes to the other such as a general obligation that work is to be undertaken in return for wages.

How to assess whether you have an employment contract
It may be easy for you to point to a document and highlight terms that show that there is an employment contract. However in factually complex situations you will need to know how a Tribunal will assess whether or not you have an employment contract in order to make effective submissions.

To show that there is an employment contract you must show that an agreement was made, what the terms were, and that these terms demonstrate that it is an employment contract. Gather all the evidence you can to back up your position. It will never be enough to assert that something existed, happened or is true. For an assertion to be accepted by the Tribunal you will have to provide evidence in support. In addition to documents and the like, evidence can also consist of live evidence given by witnesses under oath.

The test for an employment contract is made up of a mixture of factors, the exact combination of which will depend on the facts of each circumstance. These factors include whether work is done for remuneration, whether there was sufficient control by the employer for there to be an employer-employee relationship, and whether the other terms are consistent with it being an employment contract.

The Tribunal will look at a number of factual issues. It will consider factors such as whether you employ people, use your own equipment, receive paid holidays, can be disciplined by the employer and other factors such as whether you are able to exercise practical control and

legitimately make a further profit if you provide services in an efficient way.

If you supply a replacement worker when you cannot work, have no paid holiday, receive money for tasks done rather than wages, don't belong to the company pension scheme and are expected to provide your own tools, the Tribunal may well decide you are not an employee. If, on the other hand, you receive wages, have paid holidays, work under a manager who allocates work to you, and are a member of the company pension scheme, the Tribunal is far more likely to find that you are an employee. The Tribunal ought to consider the economic reality of the situation.

Disputes such as whether or not a person is an employee often arise where a person is a temporary worker or a home worker. Where there is a regular expectation of work, an employment contract may well be found. To be clear about your status it will be necessary to check current case law. An employer may well ask for a preliminary hearing to deny that you are an employee.

Employment contracts are not written down in a single

document. They may be made orally and be fleshed out in writing later. Alternatively they could be contained in several documents. Certain terms are implied by custom into them or in order to give a contract proper effect. Other terms are incorporated by statute. The main terms must be supplied in a statement to the employee within two months of beginning work. This written statement of terms is evidence of the main provisions of the contract but is not the actual contract.

The written statement of particular terms of your contract
This must be given to you within two months of the commencement of your employment. It must contain the names of you and your employer, state when your employment began and state when your 'continuous employment' began. As will be seen, your 'continuous employment' could have begun with an associate company or with a previous employer.

In addition, the following terms should be stated:

- the rate at which you are paid and how often you are paid
- what your hours of work are and how they are expected to be fulfilled
- details of your holiday allocation, which give further information on your holiday pay and company policy in relation to public holidays
- company policy if you are sick or injured and details of arrangements for sick pay
- details concerning your pension scheme
- the length of notice which you must give to terminate your employment contract
- a description of your job and the title of the position you hold

- if your job is not permanent, details of its duration
- where you will be expected to work
- any relevant collective agreements which import terms into your contract
- if you are to work outside the UK, further information on pay and the terms relating to your return to the UK
- details or reference to the disciplinary and grievance procedures that are to apply between you and your employer.
  [*Employment Rights Act 1996, section 1*]

If you are not provided with a written statement, or you dispute that the terms are those that you have agreed to, make a complaint to the Tribunal. If it finds that the statement should have been given or requires amendment, it may go on to state what terms should be incorporated into the agreement.

Terms which are implied into a contract

Certain terms are commonplace and implied by virtue of being customary in that particular area of work. In addition, a term may be implied in order to give the contract 'business efficacy', that is in order to ensure that the desired effect of the contract is produced. There are implied terms than an employer will provide a safe system of work, treat the employee fairly and not destroy the relationship of mutual trust and confidence.

There will be often be an implied term that you will act responsibly. You will be expected to obey your employer's instructions, keep confidential information confidential, and give reasonable notice of your intention to leave your job in the absence of a specifically agreed term.

Seek advice at an advice centre or a law centre if you have been treated badly by your employer. Ask what implied terms your employer might be said to have broken. Careful drafting of implied terms may help you formulate a claim for breach of contract or unfair dismissal more effectively.

Terms which are expressly stated

These are the terms that have been written down or agreed in conversation. There may be several documents in which express terms are found. These include the written statement of terms, a letter making you the job offer and any subsequent document agreed by you and your employer. An express term in a written document may incorporate a further written document such as a disciplinary code, a grievance procedure or a collective agreement.

The role of collective agreements

These are agreements made between trade unions and employers. Any terms that apply between the individual employee and the employer will be deemed to have been incorporated. If the collective agreement is modified in respect of these provisions, your contract will be up-dated accordingly. Provisions relating to a collective agreement can be incorporated expressly or by implication. Terms arising out of a collective agreement may well bind you even if you are not a member of the union that negotiated them.

Terms incorporated by Parliament

A number of statutory terms are incorporated into an employment contract. For example, there is a minimum wage policy established under the *National Minimum Wage Act 1998*. Anyone who is paid less than the statutory amount to which he is entitled can complain and will be able to sue for breach of contract in a County Court or Tribunal. From October 2000 the main rate for adults over 22 is £3.70 an hour.

In addition, there are new provisions governing the organisation of working time under the *Working Time Regulations 1998*. These govern matters such as how many hours you work in a week, the breaks you ought to have in a normal working day, how much annual holiday you are entitled to and what period of time you must have off from work in a given week.

Renegotiating terms of an employment contract

For the terms of your contract to be varied, both you and your employer must agree to the variation. If an employer varies unilaterally, you will need to grasp what constitutes agreement to the variation of your employer and what constitutes rejection.

When your employer varies the terms, your contract to your detriment, you may not be able to stop work in protest because you are dependent on your job for your income and have no guarantee of being able to find alternative work quickly. A continuation of work may constitute acceptance of the contract. To avoid this, if you must continue working, make it clear in writing that you are working without accepting the variation. Do not leave matters more than a month. The alternative is to make a claim for breach of contract in a Court or to resign and make a claim for constructive dismissal (a form of unfair dismissal) in the Tribunal.

It is possible to bring a claim against an employer for breach of contract whilst you are still employed by him. However such a claim, unless it is for unpaid wages, will have to be brought in the High Court or a County Court.

Wrongful dismissal

This is a form of breach of contract that occurs when an employer dismisses an employee and in doing so acts in breach of contractual or statutory obligations to give the proper period of notice. If an employee has suffered a loss arising out of his employer's actions he can claim for wrongful dismissal. In this section we will be looking at:

1. Notice
2. Gross misconduct
3. Counter-claims by the employer
4. Damages
5. Other remedies
6. Wages
7. Claims

Notice

It is your right, by the terms of your contract or by statute, to be given proper notice. This right to notice will not be upheld at a hearing if your conduct is deemed to constitute 'gross misconduct'. An employer who dismisses an employee summarily without notice may allege gross misconduct and thus avoid having to give proper notice and payment for the notice period.

Many employees have fixed term contracts. If you are one of them and are dismissed without notice, you may be able to bring a claim for the outstanding period of your contractual term.

The notice period

Your contract will often specify how much notice you should be given by your employer. There is a legal minimum (see below). A contract may specify a period of notice that is longer. Check your contract and make sure you are receiving the correct period of time. Your contract may also specify that payment in lieu of notice is permissible. If so there will be a claim for a 'debt' due under the contract and not for 'damages' if your employer dismisses you without payment. However, if he dismisses you without notice where notice (but not payment in lieu) was specified, there will be a breach of contract and loss, and thus a claim for damages. A failure to make a payment for dismissal in respect of the notice period upon dismissal forms the basis for a claim of wrongful dismissal.

Length of employment	Length of notice
Up to 4 weeks	No notice
4 weeks up to 2 years	1 week
2 years up to 12 years	1 week for each full year worked
12 years plus	12 weeks

[*Employment Rights Act 1996, section 86*]

Gross misconduct

As an employee you may be dismissed summarily (without notice) for gross misconduct. An employee found to commit gross misconduct has lost the right to be paid for the period of his notice and thus cannot succeed in a claim for wrongful dismissal. Typical examples of gross misconduct include:

- Theft at work
- Disobedience
- Behaviour that destroys the employer/employee relationship

In deciding what constitutes gross misconduct, any disciplinary code used by the employer is taken into account by the Court or Tribunal. In resisting claims of gross misconduct, you should make representations to the Tribunal or Court that your behaviour was not of such a nature as to constitute gross misconduct as defined either by your employer's disciplinary code or as a matter of common sense. Where you are found to be responsible for misconduct of some kind, submit that your behaviour was not so serious as to justify dismissal.

Counter-claims by the employer

A claim can be made for breach of contract against an employee by an employer to recover damages. Such a claim can be founded on grounds such as the failure of the employee to do the work specified in the contract or for breach of an implied duty of care by him. If you sue for breach of contract for wrongful dismissal, your employer may counter-claim for a breach of contract on your part.

Once such a counter-claim has been made against you, you will not avoid it by discontinuing your action.

Damages

The award of damages

This is the most common remedy. At any hearing you should bring a schedule (list) of damages to help you to argue for the full amount of damages from a position of strength.

We will look at damages in the following way:

- Calculating how much you are owed by way of damages
- Other forms of damages
- Can I recover damages for the manner of dismissal?
- Claiming for a future pay rise and expected bonuses
- Claiming job seekers allowance after dismissal
- The effects of dismissal on pension entitlement

Calculating how much you are owed by way of damages

If you are summarily dismissed without notice and your contract makes no express provision for payment in lieu of notice, you may bring a claim for wrongful dismissal. Remember that if there was a provision in your contract for payment in lieu of notice then you will have a claim for a debt, not damages. A claim for debt is not subject to the need to deduct an amount for mitigation of loss (see below).

The amount of damages claimed is determined by the fixed period of time you would have worked had you served out your notice. Once the period for loss of earnings has been established, damages are assessed as the loss of earnings and other fringe benefits. Having arrived at this figure the Court or Tribunal will ask two questions:

1 Has there been any mitigation of loss?
2 Are damages taxed?

1. *Has there been any mitigation of loss?* You must take reasonable steps to mitigate your loss by finding alternative employment. A Court or Tribunal may deduct an amount it considers reasonable if it feels you have not made reasonable efforts to find alternative employment. You do not have to take the first job available. That said, a Tribunal is likely to find that a drop in salary, caused by taking less well paid work, will not make a new job an unsuitable one. However, if the new job is lower in status, level of responsibility or competence then it is unlikely to find that you ought to have accepted it. Any money you do earn from a subsequent job will fall to be subtracted as an amount from the sum of damages that you are to be awarded, as you will have mitigated your loss.

2. *Are damages taxed?* Damages for wrongful dismissal are assessed as net salary together with the value of any fringe benefits. They are awarded as if tax had already been deducted as the idea is to compensate the employee for any actual loss. If the amount of damages awarded is likely to be in excess of £30,000, the position changes and the award is liable to tax.

Other forms of damages

There are other situations where you may make a claim for damages for breach of contract. If your employer varies a term of your contract by offering fewer hours of work and adjusts your pay accordingly while you are still willing to work for the hours and pay of the original contract, then you are entitled to claim damages.

If a contractual disciplinary procedure was not followed before you were dismissed then the amount of time that might have been spent going through the procedure can be added to the period of notice when calculating the amount of damages that can be claimed.

Further, if you were summarily dismissed without the company disciplinary procedure being used, in breach of contract, and you would have qualified for unfair dismissal (see Wednesday's section) as you would have been an employee for a year had the disciplinary procedure been used, you may be able to claim for loss of the right to claim for unfair dismissal.

Can I recover damages for the manner of dismissal?
If you are claiming for wrongful dismissal then you cannot at present claim damages for the manner of dismissal even if your prospects of finding another job are harmed as a result. This means that you cannot claim extra damages for the particularly humiliating way in which you were treated *on dismissal* by alleging that this treatment constituted a breach of an implied term of trust and confidence. The law in this area is hotly contested and confusing. You will need up to the minute advice before you make your claim.

Claiming for a future pay rise and expected bonuses
It is possible to claim bonuses and anticipated pay rises for the period of notice you would have enjoyed but for your summary dismissal by your employer.

Claiming job seekers allowance after dismissal
Any money you receive by way of job seekers allowance during the time that notice would have run is deductible from the sum of damages in the sense that the amount

awarded is reduced to reflect payments made.

The effects of dismissal on pension entitlement
Damages that are awarded for wrongful dismissal cannot be set off against your pension.

Other remedies

In the County Court the following remedies other than claims for damages are available:

Injunction
If you are dismissed without the correct disciplinary procedure being followed it is possible to apply for an injunction to prevent the dismissal until the proper procedure has been complied with. An injunction will usually only be granted where mutual trust remains between you and your employer.

Specific performance
This is where an employer is ordered to perform some part of the contract. The courts are unwilling to enforce an employment contract if one or both of the parties is unhappy about continuing the relationship.

Declaration
If your employer is in breach of contract and you want the contract to continue to remain in force, you can apply to the court for a declaration to that effect.

Wages

Wages claims are not wrongful dismissal claims. However they are included in this section because they form a type of claim which involves a claim under the contract of employment. We will look at the following:

- If I am not paid by my employer what should I do?
- What are wages?
- What is a deduction?

If I am not paid by my employer what should I do?
Unpaid wages are debts owing to you as an employee. A claim for them can be made in the Tribunal. A claim for wages is appropriate when there is no dismissal but there has been a wage deduction.

There are two interesting differences between wage claims and wrongful dismissal claims. They are not subject to the £25,000 cap in wrongful dismissal claims. Furthermore, unlike wrongful dismissal, the employer cannot bring a counterclaim against the employee.

What are wages?
The following matters are wages:

- money paid from employer to employee including holiday pay, bonuses and commission
- maternity pay and statutory sick pay.

Pensions, redundancy payments, loan of advance wages and any money paid over to compensate for expenses do not qualify as wages.

What is a deduction?
There are some circumstances when employers can make deductions from wages:

- if it is agreed that a deduction is to be made in certain circumstances

- where there is an earnings order imposed by the court or another type of deduction authorised by statute
- deductions made lawfully, for example for a Trade Union subscription, where written consent is given
- deductions from retail employees' pay (max 10% on any working day) to cover till or stock shortages

Claims

A claim for wrongful dismissal may be brought in the Employment Tribunal or the County Court. The Tribunal is the better forum if you are also bringing a claim for unfair dismissal and/or redundancy as you can bring all your claims together. However there are drawbacks to bringing a claim there:

1. The amount of damages is limited to £25,000. In a County Court there is no limit.
2. The maximum time limit for bringing a claim is 3 months from date of dismissal. In a County Court the time limit is 6 years.
3. A remedy other than damages can only be sought in a County Court. Furthermore even a claim for damages can only be brought in the Tribunal if the employee has been dismissed. If an employee feels that his employer has acted in breach of contract but he has not been dismissed he will not be able to bring a claim in the Tribunal.

Unfair dismissal

This is the claim most commonly made by employees who have been dismissed. Compensation for unfair dismissal compensates the employee for an infringement of the *right* not to be unfairly dismissed and for loss and future losses arising in consequence. The elements of unfair dismissal are examined as follows:

1. What is unfair dismissal?
2. Your entitlement to written reasons on dismissal
3. Employer behaviour that is automatically unfair
4. The need to establish continuity of employment
5. The importance and relevance of your effective date of termination ('EDT')
6. The elements of a claim for unfair dismissal
7. What happens if you go on strike?
8. How a job may end without there being a dismissal
9. People who cannot claim for unfair dismissal

What is unfair dismissal?

Unfair dismissal claims are not dependent upon the terms of your contract. You have the statutory right not to be unfairly dismissed. This right is only available to employees. If your employer wishes to avoid a claim for unfair dismissal he may dispute the notion that you are an 'employee' in law and assert that you are an independent contractor instead.

Your entitlement to written reasons on dismissal

Employees who have been employed for a year are entitled by law to a written statement from their employer within 14 days of their dismissal. This should set out the reasons for dismissal. If it is not supplied to you on dismissal and you have requested it, make a claim to the Tribunal that your employer has unreasonably withheld it. You can also complain if the statement contains material that is untrue or inadequate.

There are two remedies available. The Tribunal can make a declaration as to what it considers were your employer's reasons for dismissing you. Further, it may award you two weeks pay by way of compensation.

Employer behaviour that is automatically unfair

There are some types of behaviour by an employer that are automatically unfair reasons for dismissal. We will look at these before moving on to types of behaviour where fairness is in issue.

The main types of behaviour by an employer that are regarded as automatically unfair involve:

- Health and safety cases
- Spent convictions
- Trade Union membership
- Maternity issues
- Certain redundancy issues

- Transfer of undertakings
- Industrial action
- 'Working time' cases
- 'Minimum wage' cases
- Public interest disclosure cases
- Assertion of statutory rights

Health and safety cases
If the main reason was related to the 'Health and Safety' work you were engaged in, or that you left the workplace, or protected yourself or others, in response to serious and imminent danger, your dismissal will be regarded as automatically unfair.

Spent convictions
If you are dismissed because you have a conviction which is 'spent', this will be automatically unfair. Many types of job are exempt from this provision. If a conviction is not spent then it may be fair to dismiss but the reasonableness of the dismissal will fall to be considered.

Trade union membership
Membership or non-membership of a trade union and

participating in the activity of a trade union is not an acceptable reason for dismissal and is automatically unfair. There is no need for one year's continuous service to bring a claim for this. Nor is there an upper age limit.

Maternity issues
If you are dismissed by reason of pregnancy or as a consequence of maternity leave, then this will be regarded as automatically unfair.

Certain redundancy issues
If you are chosen for redundancy as a result of pregnancy, childbirth, any 'Health and Safety' duty you were undertaking, asserting minimum wage or working time rights or in relation to trade union membership or activity, then one of these reasons, among others, will be automatically unfair.

Transfer of undertakings
A dismissal will be automatically unfair if it is by reason of what is known as a 'relevant transfer'. This is provided the dismissal is not for an 'economic, technical or organisational' reason concerning changes in the workforce. If the latter reason is found to be the reason for dismissal, then the employer will still have to show that dismissal was fair in all the circumstances.

Industrial action
If you take part in an official action then dismissal for this will be automatically unfair.

'Working time' cases
If you are dismissed by reason of your behaviour in asserting or relying on your rights under the *Working Time Regulations*

1998, your dismissal will be automatically unfair.

'Minimum wage' cases
If you are dismisses by reason of your behaviour in asserting or relying on your rights under the *National Minimum Wage Act 1998*, then your dismissal will be automatically unfair.

Public interest disclosure cases
If you make a protected disclosure, commonly understood as 'whistle blowing', and you are dismissed for that reason, this will regarded as automatically unfair.

Assertion of statutory rights
If you are dismissed by reason of having acted to enforce a statutory right of yours against your employer, this will be automatically unfair.

NB: Race, sex and disability discrimination
Dismissal for discrimination is not automatically unfair but is likely to lead to a finding of unfair dismissal.

The need to establish continuity of employment

To be able to exercise some of your basic employment rights you will need to show continuity of employment. For most grounds leading to a claim of unfair dismissal this period is 1 year. Your employer may try to claim that you lack enough continuity of employment to make a claim. It will be up to him to prove that point.

The date on which your employment began is usually the date on which your employment began under your contract of employment. However continuity of employment is not necessarily the same as the period of time you have been working under your current employment contract. It may also include time spent working under a previous contract for the same employer, time spent working for an associated employer and also time spent working for a previous employer where there has been a transfer of undertakings.

Matters affecting continuity of employment
If you are not at work by arrangement, then your continuity of employment will not be interrupted. Similarly, if there is a temporary cessation of work at the place where you work, then continuity will be presumed to continue. Where sickness is concerned, continuity will be preserved during 26 weeks absence after contractual sick leave. However in respect of strike action, whilst continuity is preserved, any time spent on strike does not count towards the total amount of time by which continuity is measured. Breaches in continuity will occur if there is no employment contract in effect and there is a gap longer than a week.

The importance and relevance of your effective date of termination ('EDT')

Continuity is usually measured from the moment when a relevant employment contract comes into effect. It concludes on the date that employment finishes or is terminated. This is the effective date of termination or 'EDT'. If you are given notice then your EDT will be on the day that the notice expires. If on the other hand no notice was given, and you were entitled to none, then your EDT is the date on which your employment was terminated.

If you ought to have been given statutory notice, for example on summary dismissal where there is no proven allegation of gross misconduct, then that notice period will be added on from the actual date of dismissal when determining your EDT. If you are on a fixed term contract your EDT will be the day on which that contract expires.

The elements of a claim for unfair dismissal

In this part we will be looking at the elements that make up a claim for unfair dismissal:

- What is a dismissal?
- Reasons which are given for dismissal
- The test for the reasonableness of the dismissal

What is a dismissal?
You must establish that there was a dismissal. If your employer accepts this, the Tribunal will move straight to considering the reasons given for the dismissal and its fairness or otherwise. If your employer disputes that there was a dismissal, then unfortunately the burden will be on you to prove it. There are three situations where a dismissal will occur:

1 Employment contract terminated by the employer
2 Fixed term contract expires without being renewed
3 Employee terminates contract where entitled to as a result of employer's conduct ('constructive dismissal')

1 *Employment contract terminated by the employer* This can be dismissal with or without notice.

2 *Fixed term contract expires without being renewed* The non-

renewal of a fixed term contract counts as a dismissal even if that contract contains a provision for early termination by notice.

3 *Employee terminates contract where entitled to as a result of employer's conduct ('constructive dismissal')* This occurs where an employer acts and causes a serious breach of the employment contract enabling the employee to resign. If the employer merely acts unreasonably, this is not enough. In an employment contract there are implied terms such as that of mutual trust and confidence, of an employer's duty to provide a safe system of work and of a duty to treat the employee fairly. You should consider whether such a term ought to be implied into the contract and further whether it has been breached. There will also be express terms which are also capable of being breached, such as the number of hours worked and the amount of wages to be paid where it will be clear if there is a breach. Other examples of a breach of contract include verbal abuse, bullying and failure to provide support.

If you resign when you believe that your employer has acted in breach of contract you should make it clear why you are resigning. If you delay too long then it be taken that you have accepted the employer's breach of contract as if it is an agreed variation. If you resign in a moment of temper, quickly retract you resignation, and are not allowed back to work, a Tribunal will probably find that you were dismissed.

Reasons which are given for dismissal
Once it is established that there has been a dismissal, the next stage is to establish the employer's reason for the dismissal. When it comes to establishing the reason for this, the burden falls on the employer.

If an employer dismisses you for a reason that does not come within the list of categories of potentially fair reasons for dismissal (known as *prima facie* reasons), then the dismissal will be unfair. The employer has the burden of proving that it was for a prima facie fair reason. The categories of reason that are considered prima facie to be fair are:

1 The conduct of the employee
2 Statutory restriction
3 Redundancy
4 The capabilities or qualifications of the employee
5 Some other substantial reason

1 *The conduct of the employee* This includes behaviour at work and also when you are not at work if your conduct outside work has a bearing on how you perform at work. Misconduct at work includes matters such as dishonesty and disobedience. In addition, behaviour outside the workplace may include criminal activity.

Where an accusation of criminal activity is made against you, your employer must have a sincere and reasonable belief that you were engaged in such activity. In any inquiry or disciplinary hearing, you should be given an opportunity to make representations. Your employer must have a specific allegation, have conducted a reasonable investigation and have given you the opportunity to make representations. He must also have decided that he believes that there are reasonable grounds that sustain the allegation and that dismissal is reasonable to deal with the situation. It can seem as if dismissal is a natural consequence of criminal behaviour but you should guard against losing your self-esteem. If you feel that you are good at your job and that your performance has not been affected by your behaviour you should say so. If you are dismissed because of disobedience through failure to obey instructions you should argue that you had good reasons for not obeying or that dismissal was not an appropriate sanction.

2 *Statutory restriction* If there is a restriction or duty arising out of a new statute that means your employer is no longer able to employ you, then it will be prima facie fair, subject to the further test of whether it is reasonable, for him to dismiss you. However, your employer should try and find you another position within his company or a related one.

3 *Redundancy* Not all redundancy situations are fair. It will depend on how the employer has acted in deciding and organising the redundancy. With the exception of the redundancy situations that are automatically unfair, other dismissals for redundancy will be considered in the light of whether the employer has acted reasonably in making redundancy the ground for dismissal. In deciding this, a Tribunal will consider whether the employer warned employees and unions in good time to allow alternatives to be explored, consulted unions as to the criteria and selection for redundancy, made selections fairly, considered representations and explored the possibility of offering alternative employment.

4 *The capabilities or qualifications of the employee* This covers the skill and health of the employee, as well as qualifications including degrees, diplomas and technical qualifications. Capability embraces ill health and incompetence. If dismissing on grounds of ill health, your employer should take pains to consult you, to obtain a medical report from

your GP and to have you medically examined by consent if appropriate. Furthermore, he should to make efforts to see if alternative employment is available within the company or an associated company. Otherwise the dismissal may be unfair.

If your competence is in issue you should be given the opportunity to improve before a decision to dismiss is made. If it transpires that you lack the qualifications for your job then a dismissal may not be the only outcome. Argue that the lack of possession of this qualification has not affected your job performance and that your dismissal was an over-reaction.

5 Some other substantial reason This category includes business-based decisions to vary an employment contract or dismiss employees on grounds such as necessary economies. It also includes situations where there has been a breakdown in relations between the employer and the employee. In addition, while a dismissal upon a transfer of undertakings is automatically unfair (see above), it may be prima facie fair if it is for an 'economic, technical, or organisational' reason.

Where changes are unilaterally made to your employment contract and you resign claiming constructive dismissal, your employer may state that the changes were for a reason such as business reorganisation. If the Tribunal accepts this, you should still argue that your dismissal was not fair in all the circumstances.

The test for the reasonableness of the dismissal
The Tribunal will have to consider whether the employer acted as a reasonable employer would have done. This test applies to the reasons for dismissal considered in the five categories above.

The issue of reasonableness is governed in the following way:

> *The determination of the question whether the dismissal is fair or unfair, (having regard to the reason shown by the employer) –*
>
> (a) depends on whether in the circumstances (including the size and administrative resources of the employer's undertaking) the employer acted reasonably or unreasonably in treating it as a sufficient reason for dismissing the employee, and
> (b) shall be determined in accordance with the equity and the substantial merits of the case.

This is drawn from the *Employment Rights Act 1996, section 98(4)*. The Tribunal will look at the reason for the dismissal. It will look at the circumstances, which include both the factual circumstances of the dismissal and the size and resources of the employer, to see if in these circumstances the employer has acted reasonably or unreasonably in treating the reason he has given as sufficient for dismissal. All relevant factors relating to the procedure used to dismiss and the potential for providing alternative employment will be taken into consideration. The burden of proving fairness or unfairness rests on you and your employer equally.

At this stage the process by which the dismissal was made is considered. This means that if your employer did not offer you alternative employment where appropriate or did not follow a just procedure in making the decision to dismiss, then a finding of unfair dismissal may follow.

The Dismissal Procedure

A Tribunal will expect your employer to have followed a fair and just procedure in taking the decision to dismiss.

When looking at the procedure followed to see if it was fair, you should give consideration to the following matters among others:

- Were you given an opportunity to explain yourself?
- Were you shown any papers or material evidence that was used in the making of a decision by your employer?
- Was there a satisfactory investigation into the matters behind the complaint?
- Was there a proper hearing and, if so, was there an opportunity to appeal?

Consider what ought to have been done according to the principles of natural justice and make your submissions accordingly. For example, if you were involved in a dispute with another employee and that employee is then involved in deciding what disciplinary measures should be taken against you, you should make a submission that you have not had a fair hearing.

At any disciplinary hearing, you should know its purpose, whether dismissal is being contemplated, who is present and you should have the opportunity to be represented if you desire it. In addition you ought to know the case against you, have the opportunity to question anyone giving evidence, and to be able to present witnesses yourself. Those conducting the hearing should listen to both sides of the argument to any mitigation (further reasons for lenient treatment if a disciplinary offence is found to have occurred) and inquire to see if there is any further evidence that may be of use before reaching a decision.

Not all disciplinary matters necessarily lead to dismissal. For lesser disciplinary breaches the Tribunal may well expect a structured system of warnings to have been followed so that there is a preliminary oral or written warning, followed by a further written warning and finally a dismissal. There is an *ACAS Code of Practice on Disciplinary Practice and Procedures in Employment* which offers useful guidance on what should be done.

You should receive letters from your employer after each investigative or disciplinary meeting, setting out the purpose of the meeting, what was discussed and by whom, and what decisions were taken as a consequence. It is always important for your employer to keep you fully informed. A failure to do so may help you sustain a claim that you were dismissed unfairly.

An employer should have an internal appeal process so that you can appeal against a finding at a disciplinary hearing. People other than those who conducted the original hearing should conduct an appeal hearing.

The reason for dismissal
Whilst it is important to consider procedure when looking at the reasonableness of the procedure used in the decision to dismiss, do not lose sight of the fact that it is also important to challenge the reasonableness of the actual or substantive reason given for the dismissal.

The test in cases of misconduct
Where misconduct is cited as the reason for dismissal,

including where a criminal offence is suspected, an employer does not have to prove an offence to the criminal standard of proof of 'beyond all reasonable doubt'. In misconduct cases there is a test known as the 'Burchell test', after the case of *British Home Stores v Burchell* 1980 ICR 303 from which the principles derive. This states by way of guidance what an employer must demonstrate when aiming to establish that dismissal for misconduct was reasonable. An employer must:

1 establish the fact of his belief (what the reason for dismissal is)
2 have reasonable grounds upon which he can sustain that belief
3 have carried out a reasonable investigation when coming to that belief.

Even if your employer believes that an allegation of misconduct can be sustained against you, this does not mean that it will be reasonable of him to dismiss you. Some misconduct matters do not warrant dismissal.

The law on procedural unfairness
By now it should be apparent that a finding of unfair dismissal can be based on two separate, although inter-related, bases. The first is where a substantive reason alleged by the employer, such as misconduct or incapacity, is found either to be unsubstantiated or unreasonable. The second basis is where a reason for the dismissal is found to be well-founded but there is an element of procedural unfairness in the way the dismissal took place. In the latter there may be a proportionate reduction in the amount when it comes to assessing compensation. The principle is based on the case of *Polkey v A E Dayton Services Ltd* 1988 ICR 142 and you may

hear reference to a 'Polkey reduction' or the like when compensation is discussed.

It is an established principle that employees should be disciplined in a consistent manner. If you receive poorer treatment than others then argue that this is unfair.

One final point: when the Tribunal make their decision their task will be to consider whether your employer acted reasonably and not whether the Tribunal itself would have acted in the same fashion.

What happens if you go on strike?

An employee has the right to claim unfair dismissal if he was dismissed whilst participating in official industrial action and he is dismissed by reason of this action. This dismissal is automatically unfair. For this provision to apply an employee will have to have participated in what is known as 'protected industrial action'.

If you are engaged in *unofficial* industrial action and you are dismissed at this time, you are barred from bringing a claim for unfair dismissal.

How a job may end without there being a dismissal

All situations where an employment contract comes to an end, including dismissals, are known as terminations. You cannot claim for unfair dismissal unless there was a dismissal.

If you end a contract by agreement with your employer, this will be a termination but not a dismissal. If you resign in a situation where there is no serious breach of your contract by your employer then, provided it is clear that you are resigning, this will be a termination but not a dismissal. In a situation where the work for which you were specifically employed has come to an end as anticipated, then again there is a termination without there being a dismissal. Finally, a contract may be frustrated, that is become impossible to perform, say through illness, and thus be terminated as a consequence.

People who cannot claim for unfair dismissal

Certain classes of employee are prohibited from bringing claims for unfair dismissal. This group includes those who have worked for less than one year (the qualifying period unless the dismissal is for an automatically unfair reason) and employees who are above the 'normal retirement age'. The latter is the age when you can reasonably be expected to retire in your class or group. In the absence of any guidance, it will be the state retirement age of 65.

If you are employed under a fixed term contract and you entered into an agreement before 25 October 1999 to exclude the right to unfair dismissal, you will be bound by this. Terms in fixed term contracts or agreements signed on or after this date which purport to exclude the right to claim unfair dismissal have no effect.

Remedies for unfair dismissal

The remedies that may be ordered are: reinstatement, re-engagement, and compensation. Compensation is the one awarded in nearly all successful cases, although technically the Tribunal should consider the others first. By the time a finding of unfair dismissal is made relations between an employer and an employee will often have broken down and so reinstatement and re-engagement are unlikely to be considered. The remedies will be considered in the following order:

1 Reinstatement
2 Re-engagement
3 Compensation

Reinstatement

This will reinstate you in your old job. A date will be given by which the order is expected to be carried out. This order is less likely to be made if you have been found to contribute to your dismissal.

Re-engagement

This order compels your employer to re-employ you. Your employer is ordered to re-engage you in employment comparable to the job you were dismissed from or in some other suitable employment. As with an order for reinstatement, there will be a time limit by which the Tribunal will expect the order to have been complied with.

Compensation

This is the usual remedy. If your employer challenges your estimates for compensation, you will need to show the evidence upon which your calculations rest to the Tribunal.

The elements of compensation are considered in the following order:

- The basic award
- The compensatory award
- The additional award

The basic award
This reflects the amount of time you have spent in employment. It is assessed with reference to the gross weekly amount you received in wages. At present it is calculated in the following way:

1 by establishing how long you have been continuously employed up until your effective date of termination ('EDT')
2 by counting back from your EDT the number of whole years you have been working during your period of continuous employment, and
3 by allowing an 'appropriate amount' for each full year of employment within your period of continuous employment.

An 'appropriate amount' is calculated as:

1 one and half weeks' pay for each year of employment you were not below the age of 41 (ie you were 41 or older)
2 one week's pay for each year of employment you were not below the age of 22 (ie you were 22 or older)
3 half a week's pay of each further year not covered above (ie when you below 22 years old when the year of employment ended).

Remember, you are reckoning back from your EDT, so the first year you should calculate is the year leading up your date of dismissal. If you were 41 on the first day of your final year of continuous employment, having worked back from your EDT, this counts for one and a half weeks' pay. If you were 40 on the day of your final year of continuous employment, working back from your EDT, this counts for one week's pay. There is a worked example of this below.

The definition of a week's wages is subject to a limit, currently set at £230. This means that even if you earn, say, £330 a week, you can only claim at the rate of £230 for a week's work. In addition, only a maximum of 20 years of work can be counted.

An award may be reduced where:

1 You have reached the age of 64; the award being reduced by one-twelfth for each full month after that age (check with an advisor for the latest case law in this area).
2 Your conduct prior to dismissal is such that it is 'just and equitable' to make a reduction. This is where your behaviour may be said to have contributed to the dismissal.
3 Your employer has already made a payment to you that is made on the basis that he would have to pay a sum for the basic award.
4 You have unreasonably refused an offer of reinstatement.
5 You were dismissed by reason of redundancy and you have received a redundancy payment.

Example

Case history:

- You work as an administrator in an office supplies company.
- Your employer terminated your employment on 14 June 1999.
- You were given six weeks' notice of termination.
- You are 43 years old when your notice expired.
- At the time of termination you were earning £320 a week before tax.
- The Tribunal finds that you were unfairly dismissed but that you were partly to blame.

Preliminary calculations:

- Your effective date of termination ('EDT') is worked out by taking the date of your dismissal (14 June

1999) and adding the six weeks' notice. This date is 26 July 1999.

- Working back from your EDT you calculate that you have been working for six years and two months in continuous employment with your employer, although you have had many jobs and promotions during that time.
- You note that your employer has correctly given you the statutory notice to which you entitled by law as you were given six weeks' notice of the termination by your employer.
- Although you had been working for £320 a week before tax, you are aware that you can only claim at the rate of £230 a week by law.

Final calculations:

- Working back from your EDT you will have noted that for two whole years of your six years you were 41 or over –

26 July 1998	Age 42
26 July 1997	Age 41

- For these years you can claim one and a half weeks' pay per year so –

$$£230 \times 1\frac{1}{2} \times 2\text{(years)} = £690$$

- For the remaining years of your employment you were below 41 –

26 July 1996	Age 40
26 July 1995	Age 39
26 July 1994	Age 38

26 July 1993 Age 37

- For these years you can claim one week's pay per year so

$$£230 \times 1 \times 4(\text{years}) = £920$$

- It total your basic award comes to £1610 (£690+£920)

Reductions:
Unfortunately you have been judged as half responsible for your dismissal and the Tribunal decide that it would be just and equitable to reduce your basic award by 50%. Thus the final amount which you are due under this head of compensation is £805 (£1610 reduced by 50%).

The compensatory award
The compensatory award is limited to a cap of £50,000.

The elements of a compensation award are:

1 Loss of wages
2 Loss of benefits
3 Loss of pension rights
4 Expenses
5 Miscellaneous elements

1 *Loss of wages* This is assessed as net wages after tax and other deductions. Calculate your loss of wages between your dismissal date (EDT) and the date of the hearing. Further, estimate the amount of wages that you may be expected to lose in the future after the hearing.

Losses before the hearing include sums such as overtime that is due to you under your contract. Losses should be calculated as the period leading up to when you find *permanent* alternative employment. Money from odd jobs or temporary work in the period before the hearing should not be deducted. If you do find permanent work a few weeks after your dismissal but before the hearing, the money you earn from this will only be set off against your losses for the weeks during which you are in your new job.

Example:

Key facts:

- The date when your notice of dismissal expired was 2 August 1999 (your EDT).
- You were earning £180 net per week after tax at your EDT.
- You found work in a new job earning £250 net a week on 6 September 1999.
- Your Tribunal hearing was held on 25 October 1999

Calculation of loss between dismissal and Tribunal hearing:

- Time between dismissal and hearing: 2nd August 1999 to 25 October 1999 = 12 weeks.
- Time between dismissal and finding new job: 2 August 1999 to 6 September 1999 = 5 weeks.
- Time between finding new job and Tribunal hearing: 6 September 1999 to 25 October 1999 = 7 weeks.
- Therefore period of financial loss = 5 weeks.
- Total loss = 5 (weeks) × £180 (net) = £900.

Although you earned £250 net in your new job and this

was more than the £180 you earned in your old job, the money from your new job can only be set off against the time you were actually in your job (seven weeks) and not against your losses for the period before you found your new job (five weeks). You can still claim losses for the total amount of net wages lost to you in the period up until you found your new job.

If you have not found work by the time of the hearing you can make a claim for future loss. The Tribunal will assess how long you are likely to be out of work in the future, what you would have been paid, and, when you do find work, how much you are likely to be paid. Figures such as a year (52 weeks) or half a year (26 weeks) are often used. This weekly figure will then be multiplied by your net weekly wage. For example:

- Your net weekly wage before dismissal is £250.
- The Tribunal estimates you will be out of work for 13 weeks.
- Therefore your loss will be £250 × 13 (weeks) = £3250.

If you start a new job at a lower wage ask the Tribunal to work out how much you are losing by accepting a job at the lower rate and the period of time this situation is likely to last before you wages return to the level you could have expected to be earning but for your dismissal.

Example:

- Your net weekly wage before dismissal is £250.
- After your dismissal you are without work for a while

before finding a new job where your net weekly wage is £220.

- Following representations made by you and your employer at the hearing, the Tribunal decide that, in the light of your experience and of the prevailing conditions in the job market, it will take you an estimated 13 weeks to return to the £250 level.
- Therefore your estimated loss for this period will be the difference between £250 and £220 (£30) multiplied by 13 (weeks). This comes to £390.

If you have not found another job by the time of the hearing you should claim for the period during which you are likely to be out of work and then further for a period of time during which you may well be employed at a lower weekly wage rate before your earnings return to the level at which they ought to have been.

2 *Loss of benefits* Claim for any benefits that are due to under the terms of your employment contract.

Sample list of benefits:

1 food or vouchers for food
2 holiday pay for the period of time for which you are receiving a compensation award
3 any subsidised accommodation
4 the value of a company car in so far as it was used for non-business purposes
5 membership of a gym and health insurance
6 bonuses or commission due under your employment contract.

3 *Loss of pension rights* There are three different types of loss that may occur.

1 Pension rights that you would have earned between your dismissal and the hearing.
2 Further future rights that you would have earned from the hearing until you retired (or could be expected to find another job).
3 Loss of any enhancement of your rights in respect of pension rights that you had already earned at the date of dismissal.

You should use the Government guide *Employment Tribunals: Compensation for Loss of Pension Rights* which is published by HMSO. In general your basic loss in respect of pension rights is worked out as the amount that your employer would have paid over the period for which the claim is being made.

4 *Expenses* Claim for any money that you have spent seeking work after your dismissal including items such as the cost of travel to interviews.

5 *Miscellaneous elements* You can also claim for the loss of the right to the statutory minimum period of notice. If you were working for over six years prior to dismissal, you would have been entitled to six weeks notice. To reach the same level of entitlement to notice in your new job, you would have to work there for six years. If the Tribunal makes an award, it is usually calculated as net wages for half the number of weeks of notice to which you were entitled.

The Tribunal may also make a separate award for the loss of statutory protection. This refers to the fact that you will have to work for one year with your new employer before you are able to make a claim for unfair dismissal. It is usually worth between £100 and £300.

Finally, there is very occasionally the possibility that a claim can be made for loss of reputation. Seek some up-to-the-minute advice before trying to make a claim under this head.

Reductions in compensation
How the compensatory award is reduced:

1 Payments in lieu of notice
2 Payments for redundancy
3 Contributory fault
4 'Polkey reductions'
5 Social security payments
6 Lack of mitigation
7 Miscellaneous payments
8 Maximum award

1 *Payments in lieu of notice* If you are given a payment on dismissal in lieu of, or for, the notice period to which you were entitled, it is unlikely that you will be able to claim compensation for this period.

2 *Payments for redundancy* If a redundancy payment is made by your employer, you must be careful that you do not claim for sums for which you have already been compensated. Where a redundancy payment is made, you will have to asses whether this payment exceeds the basic award which would have been payable. Any surplus amount by which your redundancy payment exceeds what would have been the basic award will be deducted from your compensatory award.

3 *Contributory fault* The compensatory award can be reduced in proportion to the amount that the Tribunal believes that you were responsible for your dismissal. It is the employee's behaviour in relation to the dismissal that is assessed, not his contribution to the 'unfairness' or otherwise of the dismissal.

4 *'Polkey reductions'* Polkey reductions can be made only from the compensatory award. Where there is a finding of unfairness on dismissal as a result of a procedural defect the Tribunal may go on to consider whether the employee would have been dismissed fairly had the correct procedure been followed. If the Tribunal thinks that there may have been a dismissal had a fair procedure been followed, but it cannot be sure, then it may reduce the amount of the compensatory award to reflect this doubt. If dismissal would certainly have occurred but for a procedural defect, the compensation award could be withheld completely.

5 *Social security payments* The Government may recoup benefits that you receive, from the time of your dismissal (EDT) to the date of your Tribunal hearing, from your employer by serving a recoupment notice thus reducing your award. This period of time between dismissal and the Tribunal hearing is known as 'the prescribed element'.

6 *Lack of mitigation* There is a duty on an employee to mitigate his loss after dismissal. If you find work by the time of the hearing then you will not have suffered any loss for that period during which you are in work. If you have not found work, the Tribunal may take the view that you ought to have done so and deduct an amount from the compensatory award to reflect this.

Sometimes an employer may make a payment to the employee before the Tribunal makes a finding of unfair dismissal or determines the level of compensation. If so, this amount may be deducted.

The additional award

These are made when your employer does not comply with orders of reinstatement or re-engagement. An additional award of between 26 and 52 weeks gross pay may be given. The Tribunal will take into account the extent of your employer's fault, the wages lost through failure to comply with the order, and any failure by you to mitigate your loss by seeking alternative employment.

Redundancy

Today we are going to look at:

- The circumstances necessary for a redundancy situation
- The reasons necessary for a dismissal for redundancy
- How redundancy should be handled by your employer
- Other situations that may count as redundancy
- How your employer may try to avoid a redundancy payment
- How to calculate a redundancy payment
- Wrongful dismissal, unfair dismissal and redundancy

The circumstances necessary for a redundancy situation

You must be an employee. Certain categories of employee are excluded from making a claim. These include civil servants and other public sector employees and those who have reached the relevant normal retirement age if it is under 65 or otherwise 65.

You will also need to show that you have worked for at least two years in continuous employment, that you were dismissed, and that this dismissal was for a reason that establishes it as redundancy. 'Continuous employment' has practically the same meaning for redundancy as it does for unfair dismissal with two important exceptions. You cannot count any week beginning before you were 18. Further, you must have worked in continuous employment for a minimum of two years.

The date on which your employment is terminated is known as the 'relevant date'. This is determined in the same way as the EDT in unfair dismissal cases.

You must be dismissed to claim a redundancy payment. A dismissal will be deemed to have taken place in the following situations:

1 Your employer terminates your contract.
2 Your fixed term contract is not renewed on expiry.
3 You, as the employee, terminate your contract in a situation where you are entitled to do so by virtue of your employer's conduct (as in constructive dismissal).
4 In accordance with the rule of law, an act of your employer or an event affecting him, operates in a way that means that your contract is terminated. For example, where your employer dies or goes into receivership.
   [*Employment Rights Act 1996, section 136.*]

If you are dismissed because your job has been given to someone who has been made redundant (known as 'bumping'), then you will probably be redundant.

The reasons necessary for a dismissal for redundancy

Next you must go on to consider whether the dismissal was for one of the reasons necessary for redundancy. Your employer may try to avoid being liable to a claim for a redundancy payment by claiming that these reasons do not apply. However the burden is on him to show that a reason creating redundancy is not established.

The criteria are as follows:

> An employee who is dismissed shall be taken to be dismissed by reason of redundancy if the dismissal is wholly or mainly attributable to –
>
> (a) the fact that his employer has ceased or intends to cease
>   (i) to carry on the business for the purposes of which the employee was employed by him, or
>   (ii) to carry on that business in the place where the employee was so employed, or
>
> (b) the fact that the requirements of that business
>   (i) for employees to carry out work of a particular kind, or
>   (ii) for employees to carry out work of a particular kind in the place where the employee was employed by the employer
>
> have ceased or diminished or are expected to cease or diminish.
>
> *[Employment Rights Act 1996, section 139(1).]*

Where your employer has ceased or intends to cease carrying on his business, you will be redundant. If your employer ceases or intends to cease work in the particular place where you work, then whether you will be compelled to move (by a mobility clause in your contract) or whether you will be classified as redundant will depend on the terms of your contract. Does your employment contract give your employer the ability to make you move if you wish to remain in employment with him or does it specify that you must work in a particular place thus entitling you to claim redundancy if work is no longer provided there? In some cases, a mobility clause may be implied.

Other situations to consider are where your employer expects that his requirements for employees to carry out work of a *particular* kind and, if specified, at your place of work, *have* ceased or diminished or are *expected* to cease or diminish. In attempting to assess whether work of a particular kind has diminished or is expected to diminish, the Tribunal will look at what you are expected to do under your contract as well as what you do in practice.

How redundancy should be handled by your employer

There are three fundamental things that an employer must do when he is considering redundancy:

1 consult with his employees
2 make the selection of those employees he proposes to make redundant
3 consider alternative employment for these employees.

Consultation
An employer should consult with any recognised trade union. He should also consult with employees individually and give them a reasonable time in which to be consulted and to respond. Everyone at risk should be consulted. It is particularly important that your employer identifies the correct pool of employees from which he intends to make

redundancies. If there are flaws in the process and outcome of the pool selection seems unfair, make sure you highlight them in any claim for unfair dismissal.

An employer should write a letter to the relevant employees that sets out the fact that redundancies are anticipated, the size and nature of the pool of employees being considered, and that there will a meeting (or meetings) to discuss the situation. Some employers offer voluntary redundancy to employees. This is usually a more generous package of benefits than redundancy. By taking voluntary redundancy you will not be able to claim unfair dismissal.

There are legal provisions for employees to elect representatives to participate in collective consultation. Employee elected representatives and representatives of trade unions are known as 'appropriate representatives' for the purposes of collective consultation. Your employer has a legal duty to disclose to them the key elements pertaining to the redundancy in writing. These include:

1 the reasons for the proposals
2 the numbers and description of those whom it is proposed to dismiss as redundant
3 the total number of employees of any such description employed by the employer at the establishment in question
4 the proposed method of selecting the employees who may be dismissed
5 the proposed method of carrying out the dismissals with due regard to any agreed procedure, including the period over which the dismissals are to take effect, and
6 the proposed method of calculating the amount of any

redundancy payments otherwise than in compliance with a statutory obligation.
[*Trade Union and Labour Relations (Consolidation) Act 1992, section 188.*]

The consultation process can be used to avoid dismissal by exploring alternatives. Take this stage very seriously even though it may seem difficult to muster enthusiasm when you feel as if dismissal is inevitable. As part of the consultation process there may be an opportunity to consider the selection process.

If your employer does not consult properly, or at all, then you will be able to apply for an award to cover the period you have been out of work in consequence. This usually applies to collective consultation but can apply to the consultation of individual employees in certain situations. If the Tribunal agrees that your employer has breached his legal duties or has failed to consult properly, they will make what is known as a 'protective award'.

Selection
Your employer ought to select people from the pool by using objective criteria such as 'last in, first out' (LIFO). Other factors such as absentee and disciplinary records may be used. The factors used should not include matters such as pregnancy and maternity leave, participation in health and safety matters or trade union activity which are automatically unfair for unfair dismissal purposes. If you have attempted to assert another legal right with your employer and he subsequently considers this as a factor that justifies redundancy this will also be automatically unfair. Personal factors should also not be used as criteria for

selection. If they are used such a selection will be rendered unfair.

Alternative employment

It is incumbent upon your employer to consider offering those chosen for redundancy alternative employment. If he does not do so, the Tribunal may find a dismissal is unfair. If you decline an offer and the Tribunal finds it was unreasonable of you to do so then you will not be entitled to redundancy pay. On the other hand, if you are not offered work at all when alternative employment could have been found, this amounts to unfair dismissal.

If you accept alternative employment, you have a four-week probationary period during which to consider your position. It may be that you feel that the new job is not suitable. If that is the case, you will still be able to claim your redundancy payment.

If you leave your old employment before your contractual period of notice has expired in order to take up another job, you will be at risk of losing your redundancy payment. It is always possible for you to leave earlier than your notice period permits on dismissal by way of redundancy and still keep your redundancy payment by agreeing such an arrangement with your employer.

An employer who is engaged in making redundancies should allow those who are selected for redundancy time off to look for alternative employment.

Other situations that may count as redundancy

Where you have no work or what is known as short-time work over a certain period of time, you will be entitled to a redundancy payment and can serve a notice to claim for one. An employer who wishes to resist your claim must show that you have the prospect of a minimum of 13 weeks work starting within four weeks of the notice claiming redundancy. A counter-notice denying redundancy and refuting your notice claiming redundancy must be served by your employer within seven days to have effect.

After serving your notice, you will be in a position to terminate your contract by giving notice of termination. This second notice must be served within a month of your first notice stating your intention to seek redundancy. If, during the first seven days of your first notice your employer serves a counter-notice stating that work will be provided, and there is a dispute on the facts, the matter must be referred to the Tribunal who will determine whether you have a right to a redundancy payment. If the Tribunal decides in your favour, you will then have a further three weeks in which to serve your second notice to terminate the contract in order to claim redundancy.

The relevant periods of time when, either laid-off or on short time, after which a claim for redundancy may be made are:

1 four consecutive weeks
2 at least six weeks in a 13-week period.

'Short time' is where you are working for less than half a week's pay per week.

How your employer may try and avoid a redundancy payment

If your employer makes a suitable offer of alternative employment, he will avoid liability for a redundancy payment if you either accept or unreasonably refuse. He may also offer to renew your old contract of employment. An offer of this nature, whether on the same or modified terms, if made within four weeks of the termination of your original contract, may have the effect of depriving you of the right to a redundancy payment.

How to calculate a redundancy payment

Redundancy payments are calculated according to a set formula:

1 half a week's pay for each year of continuous employment when you 18 to 21 years old, and
2 one week's pay for each year of continuous employment during the whole of which you were 22 years old and over, up until the next stage when you receive

3 one and a half week's pay for each year of continuous employment during the whole of which you were 41 years old or older.

Only complete years are counted. Weekly pay is calculated at the gross rate and is subject to a maximum amount per week of £230 at the time of writing. Include amounts for any contractual bonuses. Where applicable, you must reduce the amount by one-twelfth for each whole month worked after you are 64.

Example

- You earn £300 a week gross.
- You are 50 years and three months old when you are dismissed for redundancy on 18 May 2000.
- You began work on 19 November 1987.
- You were continuously employed by your employer for 12½ years.

On this basis how much ought you to be paid?

19 May 1999–18 May 2000
Age at beginning of year 49 + = 1½ week's pay
19 May 1998–18 May 1999
Age at beginning of year 48 + = 1½ week's pay
19 May 1997–18 May 1998
Age at beginning of year 47 + = 1½ week's pay
19 May 1996–18 May 1997
Age at beginning of year 46 + = 1½ week's pay
19 May 1995–18 May 1996
Age at beginning of year 45 + = 1½ week's pay
19 May 1994–18 May 1995

Age at beginning of year 44 + = 1½ week's pay
19 May 1993–18 May 1994
Age at beginning of year 43 + = 1½ week's pay
19 May 1992–18 May 1993
Age at beginning of year 42 + = 1½ week's pay
19 May 199 –18 May 1992
Age at beginning of year 41 + = 1½ week's pay
19 May 1990–18 May 1991
Age at beginning of year 40 + = 1 week's pay
19 May 1989–18 May 1990
Age at beginning of year 39 + = 1 week's pay
19 May 1988–18 May 1989
Age at beginning of year 38 + = 1 week's pay
19 November 1987–18 May 1988
(Not a complete year, does not count for redundancy purposes.)

- This comes to a total of 16½ weeks' pay for the 12 complete years you worked.
- Although you are paid £300 a week gross, you can only claim at the rate of £230 by law.
- This means that your redundancy payment is £230 × 16½ = £3,795.

Wrongful dismissal, unfair dismissal and redundancy

Redundancy is subject to the law of unfair dismissal. It is a prima facie fair reason for dismissal. If the procedure used and the decision made to dismiss you were unreasonable, it may be unfair.

Your employer may well try and avoid a redundancy claim by asserting that your dismissal was prompted by a business reorganisation.. However an employer who establishes that your dismissal was by way of a business reorganisation could be liable to pay compensation if the dismissal is proven to be unfair. Business reorganisation is a reason that may come within the 'some other substantial reason' category in unfair dismissal law as a prima facie fair reason. These still have to be shown to be reasonable. If it is alleged that the decision to dismiss you was for the reason of business reorganisation, this may have been made by your employer to defeat a claim for redundancy. In this circumstance you should claim for unfair dismissal as well.

Take care where a business is taken over by or transferred to another business, in what is known as a 'relevant transfer' of an undertaking, and you are dismissed as a consequence of the takeover. Redundancy may well be acknowledged. However this may not be the full extent of your entitlement. A dismissal because of such a transfer is automatically unfair. Your new employer may well try to defeat this by asserting that the dismissal was for an 'economic, technical or organisational' reason, coming under the 'some other substantial reason' category, which is prima facie fair. If your employer succeeds in establishing this reason, and you should resist this, go on to make submissions that this new reason itself is unreasonable. If the procedure and decision to dismiss you is found to be unreasonable by the Tribunal, they will find that you were unfairly dismissed.

If you were dismissed by way of redundancy as a consequence of your health and safety activities, trade union activities, or assertion of your employment law rights, such a dismissal will be automatically unfair.

When considering wrongful dismissal, unfair dismissal and redundancy together, remember that they seek to redress separate wrongs. A claim for wrongful dismissal is a claim for the payment due for the period of notice leading to the date of termination of your contract. Such a dismissal need not be unfair although it may be depending on the facts. Conversely, if you are paid a sum for your notice period there may be no claim for wrongful dismissal but your dismissal may be unfair, on substantive or procedural grounds, and you may be entitled to compensation on that basis.

Next steps

In this final section we are going to consider what steps you need to take in order to bring your own case successfully. This book is not an authoritative legal work that sets out the latest cases and discusses the difficult aspects of the law in detail. Instead its purpose is to enable you to assess your circumstances more effectively. To that end the following information will be useful in helping you to decide what to do next and who to seek advice from.

If you are a member of a trade union, see what advice they can provide. Consider seeking advice from a law centre or your local advice centre if they offer advice in employment law. If you decide to do this, book an appointment to see an advisor and use the short time you have with them wisely. Seek help in filling out an IT1 claim form if you are in difficulty with it. See if you can work out exactly what problems you are having with bringing your claim and ask your advisor for help on these points in particular. Although I have only given the information on how to find an official Law Centre or Citizens Advice Bureau in this section, there are a number of other local legal centres and advice centres around the country. Check your local phone book for more information.

I have also listed some useful books that lawyers use on occasion. Some of these may be difficult to follow but you should know where to find further information if you need to. It has been assumed throughout this book that you do not have sufficient funds to instruct a lawyer. If you do decide that you wish someone to advise or represent you, make sure you look carefully at any agreement you make to pay for this.

Among the number of ways of paying a representative or lawyer, there is a category containing no win – no fee agreements (which includes agreements known as conditional fee agreements and contingency fee agreements). Some of these agreements demand a high fee in the event of a win and you should be particularly careful to make sure you know what your liability will be. Remember, it is also possible to have a non-lawyer represent you such as an advice centre worker, a trade union representative or someone who works for private gain.

In this section there is also a list of Employment Tribunal Offices and how to contact them. Finally, I have provided some draft suggestions for filling out forms for various types of claim and a link to a website where you can find copies of the forms and more detailed information on employment law.

Law Centres

There are numerous Law Centres and legal centres providing free advice. Law Centres belong to the Law Centres Federation (LCF). Their website address is www.lawcentres.org.uk

In order to use a Law Centre you must live or work in its designated area. Most Law Centres will have at least one solicitor able to offer advice on employment law. Check the phone book for a list of the centres in your area.

Advice centres

There are numerous advice centres in England and Wales

that provide free advice. Many of them are Citizens Advice Bureaux (CABs). The address for your local branch can probably be found in the Phone Book. Failing that you can search their website for information on your local branch. The address is: www.nacb.org.uk

They also have a website that has some useful advice on employment law: www.adviceguide.org.uk

Reference books

This is a short list of works I have found to be useful.

Bowers on Employment Law, 5th edn, J Bowers, London: Blackstone Press.
A text book that sets out employment law in detailed and well written chapters.

Harvey on Industrial Relations and Employment Law, R J Harvey (ed), London: Butterworths.
This is one of the works used by lawyers. It is a looseleaf reference work containing detailed information on all aspects of employment law, practice and procedure. This is a book to consult on difficult points of law. Advisors often use *Harvey* themselves and may refer to it during advice sessions.

Tolley's Employment Handbook, 13th edn, by Elizabeth Slade QC, London: Tolley.
If you have access to a copy, it is well worth referring to. It covers a range of employment law issues including dismissal and redundancy. In addition, it includes a chapter on practice and procedure in the Employment Tribunal.

Free Representation Unit (FRU)

This organisation will take a case referred to it by a law centre or advice centre and place it on file. A FRU representative may then take the case on and conduct it for free. A case will only be taken on if an individual Representative decides to. Cases can only be referred to FRU by another agency such as a Citizens Advice Bureau or a Law Centre. If you visit an advice centre for advice, ask them if they will consider preparing your case and referring it to FRU.

Employment Tribunals

This is a list of the Employment Tribunals and the phone numbers for the Central Office and the Employment Tribunal Helpline.

Aberdeen Mezzanine Floor, Atholl House, 84-88 Guild Street, Aberdeen AB11 6LT, Tel: 01224 593 137, Fax: 01224 593 138

Ashford Tufton House, Tufton Street, Ashford, Kent TN23 1RJ, Tel: 01233 621 346, Fax: 01233 624 423

Bedford 8-10 Howard Street, Bedford MK40 3HS Tel: 01234 351 306, Fax: 01234 352 315

Birmingham Phoenix House, 1–3 Newhall Street, Birmingham B3 3NH, Tel: 0121 236 6051, Fax: 0121 236 6029

Bristol lst Floor, The Crescent Centre, Temple Back, Bristol BS1 6EZ ,Tel: 0117 929 8261, Fax: 0117 925 3452

Bury St Edmunds 100 Southgate Street, Bury St Edmunds, Suffolk IP33 2AQ, Tel: 01284 762 171, Fax: 01284 706 064

Cardiff 2nd Floor, Caradog House, 1–6 St Andrews Place, Cardiff CF1O 3BE, Tel: 029 2037 2693, Fax: 029 2022 5906

Dundee 13 Albert Square, Dundee DD1 1DD, Tel: 01382 221 578, Fax: 01382 227 136

Edinburgh 54–56 Melville Street, Edinburgh EH3 7HF, Tel: 0131 226 5584, Fax: 0131 220 6847

Exeter 10th Floor, Renslade House, Bonhay Road, Exeter EX4 3BX, Tel: 01392 279665, Fax: 01392 430063

Glasgow Eagle Building, 215 Bothwell Street, Glasgow G2 7TS, Tel: 0141 204 0730, Fax: 0141 204 0732

Leeds 4th Floor, Albion Tower, 11 Albion Street, Leeds LS1 5ES, Tel: 0113 245 9741, Fax: 0113 242 8843

Leicester Kings Court, 5a New Walk, Leicester LE1 5TE, Tel: 0116 255 0099, Fax: 0116 255 6099

Liverpool lst Floor, Cunard Building, Pier Head, Liverpool L3 ITS, Tel: 0151 236 9397, Fax: 0151 231 1484

London North 19–29 Woburn Place, London WC1H 0LU, Tel: 020 7273 8575, Fax: 020 7273 8686

London South Montague Court, London Road, West Croydon CR0 2RF, Tel: 020 8667 9131, Fax: 020 8649 9470

Manchester Alexandra House, 14–22 The Parsonage, Manchester M3 2JA, Tel: 0161 833 0581, Fax: 0161 832 0249

Newcastle Quayside House, 110 Quayside, Newcastle Upon Tyne NE1 3DX, Tel: 0191 260 6900, Fax: 0191 222 168O

Nottingham 3rd Floor, Byron House, 2a Maid Marian Way, Nottingham NG1 6HS, Tel: 0115 947 5701, Fax: 0115 950 7612

Reading 5th Floor, 30–31 Friar Street, Reading RG1 1DY, Tel: 0118 959 4917, Fax: 0118 956 8066

Sheffield 14 East Parade, Sheffield S1 2ET, Tel: 0114 276 0348, Fax: 0114 276 2551

Shrewsbury Prospect House, Belle Vue Road, Shrewsbury SY3 7AR, Tel: 01743 358341, Fax: 01743 244186

Southampton 3rd Floor, Duke's Keep, Marsh Lane, Southampton S01 1EX, Tel: 023 8063 9555, Fax: 023 8063 5506

Stratford 44 The Broadway, Stratford E15 1XH, Tel: 020 8221 0921, Fax: 020 8221 0398

Central Office of the Employment Tribunals 100 Southgate Street, Bury St. Edmunds, Suffolk IP33 2AQ, Tel: 01284 762 171

Employment Tribunals Helpline (free) 0345 959 775

Website and forms

IT1 forms can be obtained from Tribunals and the Employment Tribunal Helpline upon request. They are usually available from Law Centres and advice centres such as Citizens Advice Bureaux as well. In addition the forms can be viewed on the website given below.

www.satyricon.co.uk
This website contains Tribunal forms including the IT1, more information on dismissal and redundancy including discussion of case law, information on human rights in employment law and links to other useful employment law websites. It is maintained by the author.

Draft claim forms

Here are a few sample claims. They are illustrative only and are not intended to be authoritative. Each case will need to be pleaded according to its own facts in the light of what needs to be established.

1 Breach of contract/Wrongful dismissal
2 Unfair dismissal
3 Disclosure/Further and better particulars/Written answers
4 Constructive Dismissal leading to Unfair Dismissal
5 Redundancy and Unfair Dismissal

Breach of contract/Wrongful dismissal
[Section 11 of the IT1]
[Paul Marshall v Vegetable Wholesalers Limited]

1 The Applicant was employed by the Respondent under a contract of employment from 11 June 1998 to 6 May 1999 as a stock controller.
2 The terms of the employment contract were set out in a written statement of terms made on 12 June 1998.
3 The written statement included the following among other terms:
   i by Clause 3 the Applicant was to receive £300 net a week from the Respondent
   ii by Clause 7 the Respondent could terminate the contract of employment by giving four weeks notice in writing.
4 On 6 May 1999 the Respondent terminated the Applicant's employment immediately without giving the required notice under Clause 7.
5 In terminating the contract of employment the Respondent

acted in breach of contract thus causing the Applicant loss and damage.

PARTICULARS

6 The Applicant has suffered a loss of £1,200 net from 6 May 1999 to 3 June 1999. The total loss is £1,200.
7 The Applicant claims damages for breach of contract.

Signed: Dated:

Unfair dismissal
[Section 11 of the IT1]
[Johan Ballpoint v Pens Galore Limited]

1 I was employed under a contract of service by the Respondent as a Sales Assistant from 12 September 1999 to 16 September 2000.
2 The Respondent is a company, Pens Galore Limited, trading as a Stationery Shop. It employs ten people.
3 By a letter dated 2 September 2000 I was dismissed for misconduct with two weeks' notice.
4 The dismissal was pursuant to an internal disciplinary hearing on 28 August 2000 where I was accused of taking items from the store without permission and without paying for them for a period of six months to the beginning of August 2000.
5 I consider my dismissal to have been unfair.
6 I rely on the following matters of fact in support of my contention that I was unfairly dismissed:
(1) No evidence was presented at the disciplinary hearing to connect me to the missing items.
(2) The disciplinary hearing relied on the statement of a Mr Williams stating that I had been heard boasting

about taking the items

(3) There was a third employee, a Miss Evans, who was prepared to give evidence that the items would be found in the locker of Mr Williams. The hearing did not hear her evidence, nor did anyone from the company make an effort to investigate her allegations to determine their truth or otherwise.

(4) I was not allowed to have someone present with me at the hearing despite my request.

(5) I was not told that dismissal was a possibility at the hearing and did not find this out until I received the letter of dismissal.

(6) I was not given the opportunity to appeal the decision.

(7) I submit that my dismissal for misconduct was unfair by virtue of the fact that the evidence at the disciplinary hearing did not establish misconduct on my part.

(8) I submit that my dismissal was unfair in any event for reasons including, but not limited to, the fact that a fair procedure was not followed in the investigative and disciplinary process.

Signed: Dated:

Disclosure /Further and Better particulars/Written answers Disclosure

[Content of letter to your Respondent Employer to obtain the documents you need for your case]

Dear [x]

Re: Johan Ballpoint v Pens Galore Limited

I have looked at your IT3 and require copies of the following documents from you within two weeks of your receipt of this letter:

1 The statement of Mr Williams used at the disciplinary hearing of 28 August 2000.
2 The minutes taken at the disciplinary hearing of 28 August 2000.
3 A copy of my personnel file for the period of my employment with Pens Galore Limited.
4 The notes of investigative and disciplinary procedures used by Pens Galore Limited in respect of my employment with them.
5 The disciplinary code issued by Pens Galore Limited.

As you will be aware, if you do not disclose this material to me within two weeks as I have requested I can apply for an order to the Employment Tribunal to compel you to do so.

Yours etc,

Further and better particulars
Dear [x]

Re: Johan Ballpoint v Pens Galore Limited

The following further particulars are required from the Respondent in consequence of its IT3/Notice of Appearance:

Under paragraph 3(1)

'the Applicant was linked to the disappearance of the items from the shop by the statements of two other employees.'

Request:

Please give further full particulars of:

1 The identity of the two employees in question.

2 What they are alleged to have said.
3 All further matters taken into account as a result of their statements.

If this information is not supplied within two weeks I can apply to the Employment Tribunal for an order to compel you to do so.

[NB An request for further particulars of the identity of the two employees could usefully be accompanied with a request for disclosure of their statements they are said to have made.]

Yours etc,

Written Answers
Dear [x],

Re: Johan Ballpoint v Pens Galore Limited

Question:

1 In respect of the finding at the disciplinary hearing of 28 August 2000 that there were grounds to consider that the Applicant was responsible for the disappearance of the items from the shop, is it not correct that the only evidence relied upon was the uncorroborated statement of Mr Williams?
2 In respect of the hearing mentioned above, is it not the case that the Company failed to make use of a statement supplied by Miss Evans concerning the disappearance of the missing items?

If this information is not supplied within two weeks I can apply to the Employment Tribunal for an order to compel you to do so.

Yours etc,

Constructive dismissal leading to unfair dismissal
[Section 11 of IT1]

[Simon Smith v Edinburgh Trade Limited]

1 The Applicant was employed by the Respondent from 13 December 1995 to 22 June 2000 as a Buyer in the Coat Department.
2 The Respondent is a medium sized company employing 35 people.
3 By clause 5(1) was an express term contained in the written statement of terms supplied to the Applicant on 24 December 1995 that he would be consulted on buying policy and would be a member of the managerial committee responsible for buying coats.
4 It was an implied term of the contract of employment made between the Applicant and the Respondent that there was mutual trust and confidence between the parties.
5 From the beginning of May 2000 the Respondent acted in a way that unilaterally varied the contract by:
   (1) failing to consult him on changes in coat buying policy for the forthcoming year at any of the meetings held in May and June 2000;
   (2) excluding him from activities of the managerial committee responsible for buying coats from May 2000 onwards.
6 By virtue of this behaviour the Respondent acted in breach of the express term contained in clause 5(1) of the written statement of terms and the implied term of mutual trust and confidence.
7 In consequence of the breach the Applicant resigned from

the Respondent by handing in a letter personally on 22 June 2000. The resignation was expressed in the letter as being effective immediately without notice. The behaviour of the Respondent in May and June 2000, acting in breach of contract, entitled him to terminate the contract without notice.

8 The Applicant submits that he was constructively dismissed.
9 The Applicant believes that the dismissal was unfair and submits that the following facts are to be relied upon in this regard:
   (1) The Respondent's behaviour was unreasonable in that there was no evidence that the Applicant was less able in his work so as to justify excluding him in the manner outlined above in paragraph 5
   (2) There were no other extenuating factors that would allow such a policy to be considered reasonable
   (3) The Applicant had received the Company award for service in the year prior to April 2000
   (4) The Respondent supplied no reason for the exclusion of the Applicant in the manner outlined above in paragraph 5 despite repeated requests from the Applicant.

Signed: Date:

Redundancy and unfair dismissal
[Section 11 of IT1]

[Jenny Uphill v Bletherington Jobs Limited]

1 The Applicant was employed from 20 May 1994 to the 12 June 2000 by the Respondent as a Recruitment Consultant.
2 The Respondent is a small company in business as an

employment agency in Highgate, London employing eight staff.

3 There was an agreed redundancy procedure policy available for inspection that was referred to in the written statement of terms supplied to the Applicant on 25 May 1994.

4 On 1 May 2000 the Applicant was informed in a letter sent by the Respondent and signed by Oswald Bletherington, Managing Director, that she was to be dismissed by reason of redundancy from 12 June 2000.

5 The Applicant has not received the statutory redundancy pay due to her and this is due for the sum of £1,800.

6 Further and/or alternatively, the Applicant was unfairly dismissed.

7 In support of the claim that she was unfairly dismissed the Applicant relies on the following facts:

   (1) She was not redundant as the work she was doing had not ceased, diminished, nor was it expected to do so.

   (2) The Redundancy Procedure was not followed by the Respondent who therefore acted in breach of the Redundancy Procedure and unfairly by:

      (a) making no attempt to select a pool of employees from which to select people for redundancy

      (b) failing to consult the Applicant with regard to the proposal to make her redundant

      (c) failing to consider other employment within the company for the Applicant.

Signed: Dated:

NOTES